How to use this book

Follow the advice, in italics, given for teachers on each page.
Praise *the children at every step!*

Detailed guidance is provided in the Read Write Inc. Phonics Handbook

8 reading activities

Children:
- *Practise reading the speed sounds.*
- *Read the green and red words for the story.*
- *Listen as you read the introduction.*
- *Discuss the vocabulary check with you.*
- *Read the story.*
- *Re-read the story and discuss the 'questions to talk about'.*
- *Re-read the story with fluency and expression.*
- *Practise reading the speed words.*

Speed sounds

Consonants   *Say the pure sounds (do not add 'uh').*

f (ff)	l (ll)	m	n	r	s	v	z (s)	(sh)	(th)	ng nk
b	c k ck	d	g	h	j	p	qu	t	w wh	x	y	ch tch

Vowels   *Say the sounds in and out of order.*

at	hen	in	on	up	day	see	high	blow	zoo

*Each box contains one sound but sometimes more than one grapheme. Focus graphemes are **circled**.*

Read in Fred Talk (sounds).

s<u>h</u>ip   peg   leg   hen   pet   box   grab

o<u>ff</u>   wi<u>ll</u>   fix   his   <u>th</u>at   is

Red words

he   s<u>ai</u>d   no   my   I

Vocabulary check

Discuss the meaning (as used in the story) after the children have read each word.

definition:

peg leg	*wooden leg*
cash box	*money box*
grab	*snatch (I will grab that cash box)*
gulp	*to take a big swallow*

Punctuation to note in this story:

Black Hat Bob Red Hat Rob	*Capital letters for names*
This Get He	*Capital letters that start a sentence*
.	*Full stop at the end of each sentence.*
!	*Exclamation mark used to show anger and surprise*

Black Hat Bob

Introduction

Pirates are sailors who steal from other ships. This story is about a friendly pirate (well friendlier than most) called Black Hat Bob. He has an enemy called Red Hat Rob (Robb-er!). Red Hat Rob wants to steal Black Hat Bob's money that he keeps in a cash box.

Will he succeed?

Story written by Gill Munton
Illustrated by Tim Archbold

Black Hat Bob
is on his ship.

This is his peg leg.

This is his pet hen.

This is his cash box.

This is Red Hat Rob.

"I will grab that cash box," he said.

"Get off my ship!" said Black Hat Bob.

"No," said Red Hat Rob.

"I will not."

"I will fix him,"
said Black Hat Bob.

Biff biff

Gulp!

Questions to talk about

FIND IT QUESTIONS

✓ Turn to the page

✓ Read the question to the children

✓ Find the answer

Page 8-9: What does Black Hat Bob keep on his ship?

Page 10: What does Red Hat Rob say to himself?

Page 11: What does Black Hat Bob say to Red Hat Rob?

What sort of voice does he use?
(angry / furious / shouting)

Page 13: Who wins?